T0194315

TWENTY-FOUR

A Devotional for Leaders

PERRY FLETCHER

TWENTY-FOUR
A DEVOTIONAL FOR LEADERS

Scripture quotations marked KJV are from the Holy Bible, King James Version (Authorized Version). First published in 1611. Quoted from the KJV Classic Reference Bible, Copyright © 1983 by The Zondervan Corporation.

iUniverse books may be ordered through booksellers or by contacting:

iUniverse
1663 Liberty Drive
Bloomington, IN 47403
www.iuniverse.com
1-800-Authors (1-800-288-4677)

ISBN: 978-1-6632-0323-6 (sc)
ISBN: 978-1-6632-0324-3 (e)

Print information available on the last page.

iUniverse rev. date: 06/23/2020

Book Dedication

All my life I have stood on the foundation that my mother laid for me as a very young boy. That foundation is defined from the premise that in whatever you do, make sure you do you very best. In the profession that God allowed me to serve, for 19 years and counting, I've always tried to do my very best. That profession, although it's how I make a living, has never been a job for me. Every day that I have been blessed to be a coach has been a day of fulfilling my purpose.

Because God has given me the insight to pen these thoughts, I want to dedicate this devotional to every athlete I ever coached in the game of basketball. Starting with the Alcorn State Lady Braves, who gave me confidence as a coach; the Alcorn Braves, who gave me courage as a coach; the Morton Lady Panthers, who showed me how to be a father as a coach; the Morton Panthers, who showed me how to be a mentor as a coach; the Forest Bearcats, who showed me how to be successful as a coach; the Murrah Mustangs, who showed me that I belong as a coach; the Newton Lady Tigers, who showed me how to be a champion as a coach; and lastly, the Terry Bulldogs, who showed me it's nothing more important than family as a coach.

It's impossible for me to list every athlete I have ever coached, but that does not mean your name is not listed in my heart. It's because of you that I'm the leader that I am. I know

I was far from what you deserved as a coach. You could have easily had someone more qualified. However, I can't thank you enough for the effort you gave me and your respectable team. You helped me to understand that "Great Players Make Good Coaches." It's no way I can take the credit for the success I've had as a coach without giving the credit to who deserves it the most- ALL OF YOU...

I love all of you and I pray you accept the dedication of this devotional in your honor as my way of saying thank you. As we always say, Family 4 Life!!!

Acknowledgements

Lord,

There would be no me if you did not say "Let there be". For that, I give you all the honor and all the praise. It is now and forever that I acknowledge you as the Lord of my life. I pray this devotional will bring glory to your name and your kingdom. I'm so thankful for the grace you have extended to me and the mercy you have shown me. There are not enough tongues nor words for me to say thank you for all you have done. It is my prayer that my life will continue to serve as a living sacrifice unto you, which is my reasonable service. I love you and you will always be my EVERYTHING.

My Family,

Rufus and Linda Bland, thank you all for being God's greatest gifts, parents. You all have supported me with unwavering support through every endeavor I've embarked upon. Your love has truly been the heartbeat that has sustained me throughout my life. I will always love you and forever stay grounded.

My Son,

Champ, I'm so grateful God gave me the opportunity to be your dad. Throughout my coaching career, I know it has been challenging for you to share your dad with so many others, but through it all, you have never complained. For that, I say thank you. I pray you know that you are still daddy's man and you will always be the number 1 priority in my life.

The Ship Family,

Greater New Friendship Church Family, thank you for submitting to me as your leader. I get so overwhelmed every time I think about God entrusting me to lead such a wonderful group of people. It's my desire every day that I can continue to walk in humility and integrity as I lead you to the destiny God has bestowed upon you.

To Monica Kincaid,

Thank you for your effort in helping to develop the themes for this journal. I couldn't have completed this project without your insight and support. I'm forever grateful for your efforts.

My Wife,

I saved the best for last but certainly not the least. Monya, I never would have made it, never could have made it, I would have lost it all but now I see you were there for me. And I can say, I'm stronger, I'm wiser, I'm better, much better. When I look back over all we have been through, I can see that you were the one I held on to. To the world, those words are just lyrics from Marvin Sapp, but to you, Monya, they should register a little more meaning. Through all the ups and downs, some way, we weathered the storm. It's nothing I can do to repay you for risking your life to save mine. I'm forever in debt to you for how you willed me back to life when COVID -19 should have killed me. Since I have no money to repay my debt, LOL, it is my vow to continue to love you for the rest of our life.

INTRODUCTION

Lara Smith quoted in an article the following:

"Whenever the Angel Number 24 appears again and again in your life, you have the assurance from archangels that they are with you in enhancing your optimism and self-reliance. Your attempts and hard labor of the past have resulted in ensuring a strong base for your desires. You have to follow it up with self-belief and insight. Angel Number 24 is assuring you that whatever you are doing is in the right direction."

Mrs. Smith's commentary on the number 24 further solidifies my attachment to this number. Long before I ever read Mrs. Smith's explanation of 24, in 1993, in the Bettye Mae Jack Middle School Gymnasium, in Morton, MS, the number 24 and I were united. This relationship would be an everlasting bond that I still carry today, with hopes of passing it to my only son, PJ. 24 is the basketball number I chose to wear in junior high, high school, and college. My reasoning for choosing the number 24 was because it was the closest number available to 23. We all know the number 23, The G.O.A.T., Michael Jordan, the greatest of all time (in my opinion). I figured since I couldn't get my favorite player's number, I would get the closest to it. Every time I put my uniform on, in every game, in every practice, I was motivated to do my very best because I wanted to live up to the significance of #23. I wasn't nearly the athlete nor player that Michael was but, in my mind, I had to be on my best game because the number 24 was too close to the number of the G.O.A.T. In no way did I want to bring shame nor disgrace to the legacy of #23.

Now, here it is 27 years later, and the #24 has resurfaced. When my career ended as a player in 2001, the Lord opened the door for me to coach the game that saved my life. After I made the transition from coaching on the collegiate level to coaching high school, I experienced a low point in my career as a head coach. I was doing all I could do to coach my athletes to be successful and it seemed like my efforts were all in vain. So, each week I would choose a bible verse to meditate on to get me through the week. Then, on the weekend, I would write a response to the revelations I received from the verse. Believe it or not, this regimen helped me get through a very dark place in my life. During this time, my purpose for writing was nothing more than devotion and a means to an outlet for me. After a few years, these writings, which were in a notebook, got lost in the shuffle in my office. It wasn't until my tenure, at Forest High School, was up and I was packing up my office that I discovered the notebook. I sat in my chair and begin to read and reflect on the entries and my heart began to swell with emotions. Even though when I wrote these entries, I was writing from a very dark place, I realized the contents were filled with much light. The spirit spoke to me and said, "the same way these words have given you life, they can do the same for others".

As I considered the notion, I talked myself out of it because I felt it wasn't enough entries to be of any help. The spirit spoke to me again and said, "it's not quantity that blesses, it is quality". I came up with another excuse. I said it would cost too much for such a minor project. The spirit spoke a third time and said, "cost didn't keep Jesus from going to the cross". I couldn't argue with that. I begin to wrestle with the thought of what would be the title. I thought about A Coach's Devotional, Mental Boot Camp, Leader's Manual, A Word for Difficult Days but nothing just "clicked". The spirit spoke yet again and said, "how many entries do you have?". I counted and it was 24. It was then that I realized it was the #24 that inspired me to be my best even when I wasn't the best. From that revelation the title of this book was birthed...24.

So, I present "24" to you, to do exactly what it did for me. Simply encourage you to be your best even when you don't feel you are the best.

What Really Matters

By Coach Perry Fletcher

*And whatsoever ye do, do it heartily as
to the Lord, and not unto men.*

Colossians 3:23

In the life of a coach it is easy to find yourself caught in the battle of tug of war within your career. So often you want to do a good job of improving your team and impressing your fans that your passion for coaching turns into a pressure to succeed. My friend, if you find yourself in that mode, you are in a very unhealthy place for your life as a coach and as an individual.

I understand your M.O. is to win games and ultimately win championships, however, that particular M.O. shouldn't alleviate your passion for the game. Many coaches begin their career with one goal in mind; that's being the best they can be as a coach and as a mentor. Somewhere along the way with all of the stressors, attitudes, and emotion that come with the job, that mindset tends to be unfueled.

It can be discouraging when day in and day out, you empty yourself into the lives of those you are leading for their personal benefit and to your return you are left depleted with no one to pour back into you. In many cases there is even no gratitude shown for the sacrifices you make on a continuous basis. As a coach, you are looked to as not only a leader, but in many instance a parental figure. This particular perspective adds a different element to your responsibilities. Now, not only must you provide skills to build your team as athletes but you must model and implement life skills to help develop them into positive citizens.

As you consider the latter expression, it's imperative that your demeanor as a coach is governed by Paul's writings in Colossians 3:23. The work we do as coaches is not evaluated or measured by people. We must attend our job as coaches and leaders as though we were accounted to the Master and not Man. When we develop the attitude that the work we do in the life of others must only meet the approval of God, then we can better handle the pressure from our peers. We can never be great enough to please those in the stands but if what we do is from the heart, we will please the one above the clouds.

DAY 1

What Really Matters

By Coach Perry Fletcher

MEMORY VERSE: COLOSSIANS 3:23 (WRITE)

_____

_____

HIGHLIGHT PLAY

"We can never be great enough to please those in the stands but if what we do is from the heart, we will please the one above the clouds."

1ST HALF (OBSERVATION)

+ What means more to me, building championships or building character?

_____

_____

+ Do those that I'm leading share the same passion that I have? If so, in what ways?

_____

_____

Half Time (Evaluation)

- Does my attitude reflect Paul expressions in Colossians 3:23?

  _____

  _____

- In what ways can I improve my attitude toward those I'm leading?

  _____

  _____

2ᴺᴰ Half (Prayer Time)

Lord God, when I'm tempted to lose focus on my calling, gently remind me of "what really matters". I am a light in a dying world. My prayer is that I will daily surrender my ways, my actions, and my life to you; all for your glory. Amen.

DAY 2

Facing the giants

By Coach Perry Fletcher

"Fear thou not: for I am with thee: be not dismayed: for I am thy God: I will strengthen thee; yea, I will help thee; yea I will uphold thee with the right hand of my righteousness."

Isaiah 41:10

Many times coaching can lead you into some hostile environments. This hostility is usually brought on by the passion of the game and the importance your sport may bring to the town. So whenever you walk into your arena of competition, all eyes are upon you. These eyes are not just to see your attire, but to see if you will succeed or to see if you will fail. In many instances, these eyes are not there to support you, but they are there to be judgmental. The sad reality is that no one seems to realize that no matter how prepared or unprepared you are as a coach, you can't score one basket, throw one touchdown, kick a single goal, hit a homeroom, score one winning put, bowl a strike, hit an ace for that all lies in the power of the player. In knowing this reality, you can still be looked upon and held responsible for your athlete's performance between the lines. From the heart of a coach, this reality can be frightening and fearful. No matter how self-sufficient you may be, no one wants to hear their name scandalized, especially in the stands amongst your family.

In regards to the fear and the fright we may experience, Isaiah offer us some assurance in his writing. Whether you admit it or not, there are times the hostility you face can be fearful. Isaiah, being one of God's all-star coaches, understood that going into hostile places with great expectancy upon your every decision could bring on some fearful moments. God gave Isaiah a confidence boost by assuring him that wherever his assignment may take him, he had no room or reason for fear, because He would be with him. My fellow colleagues, when you are leading your team and God is your ultimate guide, it's no place you will go where the presence of God won't be with you. Isn't it comforting to know that after exerting all of your time, and all of your energy in preparing for your contest, God promised to be your strength in your weakness? Even if all the energy in the arena is against you, and regardless to whether we receive help from your assistants, Our God said he would help us. Knowing that you have the help of God adds a wealth of encouragement in every contest. He is able to protect and present you with power over your enemies. Knowing that God is with you gives you the liberty of enjoying what you do as a coach. It's because he is with you, you can stand tall in the face of fear because he has made your enemies be footstools.

DAY 2

Facing the giants
By Coach Perry Fletcher

MEMORY VERSE: ISAIAH 41:10 (WRITE)

_____

_____

HIGHLIGHT PLAY

"The sad reality is that no one seem to realize that no matter how prepared or unprepared you are as a coach, you can't score one basket, throw one touchdown, kick a single goal, hit a homerun, score one winning point, bowl a strike, hit an ace, for all the lies in the power of the player."

1ST HALF (OBSERVATION)

   ✦   What is the one thing you fear as a leader?

   _____

   _____

+ Do those that I'm leading share the same passion that I have? If so, in what ways?

_____

_____

Half Time (Evaluation)

+ What actions stems from fear?

_____

_____

+ In what ways can you eliminate the emotions fear from your environment?

_____

_____

2ND Half (Prayer Time)

Lord God, when I'm "facing the giants" in my life, I must know who I am in Christ. Your word in 1 john 4:4 reminds me that "the one who is in me is greater than the one who is in the world." Because I have a "he-man" in me, there is no battle, no obstacle, no evil look, or ugly words that can defeat me. Amen.

DAY 3

Keep your eyes on the prize

By Coach Perry Fletcher

"Know ye not that they which run in a race run all, but one receiveth the prize? So run that you may attain."

1 Corinthians 9:24

The art of coaching is built from your personality. Therefore whatever your personal demeanor, maybe it will be reflected in your life as a coach. With that in mind, as you prepare your team for competition, know that your team is going to take on the personality that you display as you lead them. That's why it's imperative for you to engage your athletes with a sense of urgency. Why? Every day that you are prepared for victory, someone is preparing to make you their victim.

As Paul addresses the church at Corinth, like many of us, they had gotten complacent. Due to a number of their people having spiritual gifts, they were on cruise control in their daily spiritual walk. Coaches, be mindful that we don't allow ourselves to fall victim to the same regime. Many times when your roster is filled with athletic athletes, it's easy to get relaxed in your preparation. Such action usually leads to failure. We must not allow athletic athletes to make us careless coaches. How so? It is careless when you neglect fundamental teaching and inspirational coaching because of the talent your team consist of. Talent can only get you so far. There's is an old quote that says, "It's not the best talent that wins but the best team".

When we fail to prepare our team to the best of our ability, not only are we setting our team up for failure, but we are hurting our players as well. Our athletes may be talented enough to dominate on the level we compete on, but we must keep in mind that we are preparing some of them for the next level of competition. We don't want to limit their potential because of our slothfulness. If it is our goal to be champions at season end, then every day we must prepare like champions.

Day 3

Keep your eyes on the prize
By Coach Perry Fletcher

Memory Verse: I Corinthians 9:24 (Write)

_____

_____

Highlight Play

"Every day that you are preparing for victory, someone is preparing to make you their victim."

1ˢᵗ Half (Observation)

+ Do I work as hard coaching as my players do play?

  _____

  _____

+ Do I take time to nurture and develop my players' talent or do I only utilize their present potential?

  _____

  _____

HALF TIME (EVALUATION)

- When my players leave my program, are they better than when they first was introduced to the sport?

  _____

  _____

- In what ways have I improved as a coach in my efforts to improve my team?

  _____

  _____

2ND HALF (PRAYER TIME)

Lord God, don't allow me to get side tracked and go with the flow of the game of life. My desire is to always be the one striving for the best. Do not allow me to be blinded by the wins or loses of the game but to focus on the lives I touch for your kingdom. Amen.

Day 4

It's not about me

By Coach Perry Fletcher

*"Let us not become conceited, provoking
and envying each other"*

Galation 5:26

Championship, Championship, Championship!!! Every coach's ultimate goal, no matter what sport they may coach, is to win a championship or be a part of a championship program. To accomplish this task is easier said than done. Each year, there are only a select few who can wear the crown as champion. Although this is good for some, it can be frustrating for others. Frustrating in that every coach wants to experience the unexpected shower of Gatorade, the cutting of the nets, the hoisted ride of your players, and the lifting of the hardware. In a Fruitopia world, all coaches would get those opportunities, however that is not the place we live in. The reality is that not all coaches in their tenure as a coach will ever get that experience.

With that in mind, as a coach, you can't allow the success of others to affect your psyche as a coach. Many coaches view their value as a coach based on the success they achieve. This is not good. Whether or not you produce a championship during your tenure as a coach does not validate your success as a coach. Your validation comes from you producing athletes to compete like champions and live a championship life. With the hype of sports, there are some who forget this. There are those coaches who allow the success of their programs to change their demeanor as a person and as a coach. In the book of James, chapter 4, verse 6, the word declares God opposes the proud but gives Grace to the humble. It's nothing worse than a coach that is arrogant. What generally happens is that your players will develop the same mentality that you have. Could you imagine a team full of arrogant players? There would be no room for growth because everyone would be so full of themselves. When you think you are already great, you can't' get better because you won't work as hard. Coaches. Be mindful that you don't stunt the development of your team with a conceited attitude. It's nothing wrong with being confident but make sure your confidence stems from the hard work you put in and not the product that hard work puts out.

DAY 4

It's not about me

By Coach Perry Fletcher

MEMORY VERSE: GALATIANS 5:26 (WRITE)

_____

_____

HIGHLIGHT PLAY

"It's nothing wrong with being confident, but make sure your confidence stems from the hard work you put in and not the product that hard work puts out."

1ST HALF (OBSERVATION)

+ How do I handle success?

_____

_____

+ In what ways has being successful or unsuccessful effected my demeanor?

_____

_____

HALF TIME (EVALUATION)

- ✦ What kind of example do I set for my athletes?

  _____

  _____

- ✦ Do those I'm leading show confidence or arrogance?

  _____

  _____

2ND HALF (PRAYER TIME)

Lord God, it is in my human nature to desire the sweet taste of victory in the game. As David prayed in psalm 139:23-24, "search my heart, my attitude, and my motives. Remove anything that is in me that does not give you glory." My life is not about me but it's about the gift Christ has placed in me. Amen.

I'm living to live again

By Coach Perry Fletcher

*"For physical exercise has some value, but Godliness
is valuable in every way. It holds promise for
the present life and for the life to come."*

I Timothy 4:8

Never compromise fashion for form! We now live in an age where image supersedes identity. People are more concerned with how they look versus who they really are. Because of this shift in the mental psyche of society, the same mentality exists in the coaching arena. There are those coaches who care more about producing a team of "phenomes" than they are about developing a team of character. We must be careful as coaches that we do not deduce or demoralize our athletes in efforts to bring them under submission merely to generate a win. That behavior breeds a slave mentality; where your athletes have the mind that you have to get a whip behind them to make them work. As coaches, we must be mindful of the power of influence.

Usually during the tenure in which we are responsible for our athletes, they are at a very impressionable state. Therefore, the way we instruct them will influence them either positively or negatively. So you must ask yourself, am I leading in a manner that will be beneficial for their future as a person or only their present as a player.

In our devotional verse, Paul was instructing Timothy that Godliness will prove more valuable than any other strategy you could employ. Every coach looks for the advantage or the edge over their selected opponents. Well this advantage is not found in how cunning you can curse your kids but how well you can motivate them to play above their means. So often coaches will lower their standards of integrity simply to achieve a desired result. This principle is a false method of application to achieve greatness. In all that we do, we must exemplify the attributes of God. It is from Godly attributes, we are able to gain the advantage and give our athletes the edge. How so, Philippians 4:13 declares we can do all things through Christ that gives us strength. So when you prepare your athletes with Godly attributes, not only are they equipped from physical training but spiritual as well. This, my colleagues, is the edge; giving them twice the strength they would normally have.

Day 5

I'm living to live again

By Coach Perry Fletcher

Memory Verse: I Timothy 4:8 (Write)

_____

_____

Highlight Play

"There are those coaches who care more about producing a team of "phenomes" than they are with developing a team of character."

1ˢᵀ Half (Observation)

+ Do I display Godliness in my instructions toward my team?

  _____

  _____

+ Do my players respond to me out of fear or out respect?

  _____

  _____

Half Time (Evaluation)

- ✦ Do my players display the discipline I teach in and out the playing arena?

  _____

  _____

- ✦ In what likeness do my players see me?

  _____

  _____

2ND Half (Prayer Time)

Lord, everyday it is a struggle to choose your way and not my own. Help me to point people to Christ. Help me to see that your attributes are far better than this world or my own. Amen.

DAY 6

Don't quit

By Coach Perry Fletcher

"Let us not become weary in doing good, for at the proper time we will reap a harvest if we do not give up."

Galation 6:9

Consistency, Consistency, Consistency!!! In the society we now live in, everything is ever changing. From politics to religions, nothing seems constant. Even down to the individual lives of the community, people have conditioned themselves to change. There are times when change is necessary, however change shouldn't be an alternative to doing what's right. There are a number of individuals who will compromise doing what is right if they are not getting the results they hoped for. In the world of coaching, this happens more often that none. Everybody wants instant success. Everybody seems to want to win right away. So much so until people will act immorally to achieve their goals. We must remember that success is not a quick sprint, it is more like a marathon. That's why we must remain consistent in our work ethic. To achieve greatness by any means other than hard work will only be a temporary fix. It has been said that the only place you will find success before work is in the dictionary.

In our focus verse, Paul encourages Timothy to not grow weary in doing what is right. Paul understood that it could be discouraging to continuously work in righteousness yet get empty results. Paul assures Timothy and now us that our results are not in us doing good or what's right, but it's in us not giving up. As a coach, it tends to be easy to throw in the towel. When you think about the many days of preparation you put in to make sure your team is ready for competition just to get to the contest and your team performs like they have never been in a practice. Boy, Have I been there!!! Although times like those can be frustrating and even overwhelming, you must hold to Paul's principle that your season is coming. If you look at the life of a gardener, when they have planted seeds in the ground, it takes time before what was planted begin to bloom. However, even though there are no instant results from their planting, the gardener still puts in time cultivating what they have planted. Why? Not because they see immediate results, but because they have confidence in what was inside of the seed they planted. Therefore the gardener knows in due season the seed will blossom. As coaches, regardless of unfavorable results you may receive, have confidence in knowing that in due season what you have instilled in your team will come to pass.

DAY 6

Don't quit

By Coach Perry Fletcher

Memory Verse: Galatians 6:9 (Write)

_____

_____

Highlight Play

"We must remember success is not a quick sprint, it is more like a marathon."

1ˢᵗ Half (Observation)

- What are your motives as a coach?

    _____

    _____

- Are your motives centered on producing successful athletes or producing successful lives?

    _____

    _____

Half Time (Evaluation)

- What kind of seeds has my philosophy of a coach planted?

  _____

  _____

- Does the harvest I reap coincide with the seeds I've planted?

  _____

  _____

2ND Half (Prayer Time)

Lord God, I will not be moved today by what I see, hear, or feel. I will only be moved by the word of God. I declare I will not quit or get discouraged. My focus is on you and you alone. All the good I do is working out for my good but for your glory. Amen.

DAY 7

Renew me

By Coach Perry Fletcher

"May the Lord direct your hearts into God's love and Christ's perseverance."

2 Thessalonians 3:5

What is your motivation? What drives you? What is the reason you do what you do? As a coach, ninety percent of our time is spent motivating others to be their best self. To some, motivating may seem insignificant, but to the one receiving, it is life fuel. With that being said, you must be aware that the principle of motivating can become taxing. Not only are you leading and directing others, you are depositing a piece of who you are and what you believe in into their lives. Because of this, the source of your personal motivation is very vital. It will become a burden for you to constantly give out and you have mothing or no one giving into you. Often times you can become so consumed with pushing and priming everyone else that you mistakenly neglect yourself. There are a number of coaches have found themselves wayward and/or unmotivated because of a lack of an inspirational source in their life. Having no inspirational source in your life is a hazard to your coaching personality.

The apostle Paul understood the high cost of motivating others. Being that he is responsible for writing a large part of the New Testament, if anybody could testify to being left empty from pouring out, Paul could. Now it becomes clearer why Paul penned in our key verse to allow the Lord to direct your heart. Isaiah 26 :3-4 says, "You keep completely safe the people who maintain their faith, for they trust in you. Trust in the Lord from this time forward, for in the Lord Jehovah is everlasting strength." For when you have nothing left, when you have no one to look to, you can always count on direction and motivation from the Lord. When you think about the ultimate sacrifice God made for us to have an opportunity to live beyond our sin, we can always depend on the strength the Lord provides. His strength transcends any physicality or any technicalities. Well what gives me so much confidence in the strength of the Lord?

DAY 7

Renew me

By Coach Perry Fletcher

MEMORY VERSE: II THESSALONIANS 3:5 (WRITE)

_____

_____

HIGHLIGHT PLAY

"Not only are you leading and directing others, you are depositing a piece of who you are and what you believe into their lives."

1ST HALF (OBSERVATION)

+ Who is my mentor?

    _____

    _____

+ How often do I read?

    _____

    _____

Half Time (Evaluation)

+ Is my work ethic a reflection of how motivated I am?

    _____

    _____

2ND Half (Prayer Time)

Lord God, when I am worn out with the stress and cares of the game and life, "renew me". 2 Corinthians 12:9 reminds me that your power is made perfect in weakness." Strengthen me on every hand to do the work you have called me to do. Amen.

Day 8

Who's your daddy?

By Coach Perry Fletcher

"But Jesus looked at them and said, 'With men this is impossible, but with God all things are possible'."

Matthew 19:26

Within the livelihood of coaching, you will face some difficult moments that will cause for decisive decisions. These moments will appear disastrous with no chance of recovery. For instance, you have lost your best athlete or leading scorer and you are up against your school's rival team, or your team is built like David and your opponent is built like Goliath. If you find yourself in similar predicaments, don't allow you opposition to overshadow your confidence. Whenever you are exposed to adverse circumstances, if your team is only built by manpower alone, you will fall victim to the disadvantages you are facing. It is important to remember that your team's success is not so much in the ability of an individual player, but in the principles you have taught your entire team.

Jesus makes it plain in the focus verse; what's impossible to man is possible for God. In whatever situation you encounter, don't allow your confidence to be in the hands of man. If so, then your results will be contingent on man's performance. On the other hand when your confidence is in the hands of the one that created man, then you can have the assurance that your results will be favorable and beyond failure. It is amazing to see what the power of belief can and will produce. Whatever team sport you may be a part of, it's important to believe in the team's principles that have been taught rather than the thought of failure. When your motive is to Glorify God, He is not going to allow you to fail. There is no failure in Christ.

DAY 8

Who's your daddy?

By Coach Perry Fletcher

MEMORY VERSE: MATTHEW 19:26 (WRITE)

_____

_____

HIGHLIGHT PLAY

"It is important to remember that your team's success in not so much in the ability of an individual player, but in the principles you have taught your entire team."

1ST HALF (OBSERVATION)

+ As a leader, how do I deal with adversity?

    _____

    _____

+ When the opposition I am facing is greater than my preparation, what is my message to my team?

    _____

    _____

Half Time (Evaluation)

- What can I learn from my team in adverse circumstances?

  _____

  _____

2ND Half (Prayer Time)

Lord God, you are my father. You are my daddy. I look to you to make every impossible situation possible. I look to you to do what only you can do. As I face impossible situations, I will put my faith and trust in you knowing that there is nothing you cannot do. Amen.

DAY 9

I ain't scared

By Coach Perry Fletcher

*"But he took his stand in the midst of the plot
and defended it and struck down the Philistines,
and the Lord worked a great victory."*

2 Samuel 23:12

———————————— ————————————

Every day, when you choose right over wrong, it is equated to choosing life over death. This principle is the foundation to being able to stand against opposition as well as standing for accountability. There are a number of leaders, coaches and people with a wealth of ability who are unable to get positive results due to the lack of courage. It takes courage to be able to hold others accountable for their actions and their assignments. If there is no courage, then a coward will be born. As a coach, there is no room for a coward mentality. Whenever you display cowardly attributes, your players or those you are leading will directly be affected. Therefore you must be willing to stand. Often times your stand will be unpopular and unprecedented.

It may cause you to receive ridicule and resentment, but you must not allow these attitudes to sway you from the strength of your stand.

In our selected text, notice David took a stand in the midst of his adversaries. He wasn't concerned with the aftermath or what the consequences would be. His only concern was standing up for what he believed in. This stand caused him to fight and because he was fighting for what was right, he had guaranteed victory from the Lord. Now had David no been willing to take a stand, not only would he had been a victim, but he never would have experienced the Lord's victory. It has been quoted, "If you don't stand for something, you will fall for anything." Many athletes lack structure, therefore often times discipline is not present. If you refuse to address or attend to disorderly behavior, it could lead to your team or organization demise. It doesn't take much effort to lie down but it takes strength to be able to stand.

DAY 9

I ain't scared

By Coach Perry Fletcher

MEMORY VERSE: 2 SAMUEL 23:12 (WRITE)

_____

_____

HIGHLIGHT PLAY

"It doesn't take much effort to lie down but it takes strength to be able to stand."

1ˢᵀ HALF (OBSERVATION)

+ What will be the consequences if I fail to stand against opposition?

_____

_____

HALF TIME (EVALUATION)

+ Are those I'm leading willing to follow my stand?

_____

_____

2ND HALF (PRAYER TIME)

Lord God, I will not be afraid to do what is right. For I am reminded in Matthew 7:13-14 that narrow is the way that leads to life and only a few find it. Lord, "I ain't scared" to travel through the narrow gate. Give me strength and holy boldness to lead, correct, and discipline. In Jesus' name, Amen.

DAY 10

For your glory

By Coach Perry Fletcher

> *"Whether therefore ye eat, or drink, or whatsoever ye do, do all to the glory of God."*

1 Corinthians 10:31

In society today there is a wealth of hype and hysteria linked to individual success and accomplishments. There are many people who achieve greatness with a vain purpose in mind. Meaning the motivation behind their achievements is centered around receiving self-glory for themselves. As coaches and leaders, we have to make sure that our personal ego is not larger than our team's philosophy. Whenever you make what you do about "you", your work becomes a show and not service. There is a difference. A show only makes an impression for an allotted time. When the time is up and or the game is over, everything that was done within the show will be over. On the other hand, when your work is service, whenever the time is up and or the game is over, the impression will last for a lifetime.

All the while Jesus ministered on Earth, his ministry never appeared to be about him. Everything he did was for the glory of his father. Even when his time was up and his mission was completed; because his ministry was service and not a show, after his death, people are still being impacted and impressed by what he accomplished. At no time during his season of ministry did Christ seek the spot light, however seem like the spot light always found him. When he was at the wedding in Canaan, he was just a guest with his mother but he ended up on program as the bar tender. When he was passing through Samaria, he stopped to get a drink of water and ended up the special guest in revival. In these instances, at no time was Jesus seeking glory for himself. Because of his service, the glory came to him.

In whatever we do as coaches, as leaders, as teachers and as parents, our service cannot be fueled by selfish ambition. We must be selfless in our efforts to lead. When you operate in service and not a show, it's no need to need the spotlight, the spotlight will find you!

Day 10

For your glory
By Coach Perry Fletcher

Memory Verse: I Corinthians 10:31 (Write)

_____

_____

Highlight Play

"Whenever you make what you do about "you", your work becomes a show and not service."

1st Half (Observation)

+ Is my work as a coach centered around service or the spotlight?

   _____

   _____

Half Time (Evaluation)

+ How has God received glory from my career?

   _____

   _____

2ND HALF (PRAYER TIME)

The gift of leadership is one that I did not and could not create on my own. I acknowledge that I can do and be nothing without you. My gifts have been given to me not to boast or misuse but to be used "for your glory". With my gifts, I honor you. In Jesus' name, amen.

DAY 11

Peace giver

By Coach Perry Fletcher

"These things I have spoken unto you, that in me ye might have peace. In the world ye shall have tribulation: but be of good cheer, I have overcome the world.

Galation 5:26

One of the hardest things to accept is seeing other programs or teams advance when your program has come to a halt. It's not so much that you don't want to see others succeed but it is very disheartening when you know the efforts and energy you have spent to travail your program to success only to fall short of your intended goals. Then there are always those who offer you condolences by saying, "it's always next year", or "You'll had a good run". I understand that all of that might be true, however it doesn't fill the void of your expectations. So the question arise, how do you mask the pain of failure, how do you handle the pressure of defeat, how do you deal with the emptiness of being upset? Before we can embrace the solution, we first have to deal with these realities of the latter emotions. Many people will act as though those questions don't exist. I've come to realize that when you invest yourself mentally, emotionally and physically into your work and or organizations, you will experience drawbacks if your desired goals are not reached. So the questions does remain, how do you deal with the lack of accomplishment?

Jesus is recorded by John in saying be of good cheer, He has already overcome the world. There is confidence in his words by knowing even in defeat we don't have to have a delinquent demeanor. We can have joy in knowing that the tribulation we face in the world has no power over our disposition because Christ has already conquered it. A good friend of mine, who coaches boys basketball at one of our area's high schools, validated the commentary of this particular text. During the 2013-14 season, his team dominated our district league. They ended the season undefeated in the conference giving them a conference title and a #1 seed going into the division tournament. They were the sure favorites to win the tournament. However, they lost on the first night to a team they had beaten twice by 15 plus points. If that wasn't a shocker, they lost the next night to another district team they have swept earlier. Now the team that finished #1 was going into the South State TNA as the last place team. Coach Truman was devastated and his players were demoralized. In his heart that Friday and Saturday night he felt like a sure failure and more vividly he felt like he had failed his players. Well on the following Sunday after the tournament, Coach went to his local church where he preaches. To his surprise, when he came out to the pulpit, his entire team along with their parents were all sitting in the congregation as a team standing in his support. Now you tell me, was he really a failure? Not hardly, the joy he experienced in seeing his entire team together in the house of the Lord supersedes any feeling of seeing his team in the Big House.

Success is not only measured on the accomplishments of the season but by the seeds you plant along the way.

DAY 11

Peace giver

By Coach Perry Fletcher

MEMORY VERSE: JOHN 16:33 (WRITE)

_____

_____

HIGHLIGHT PLAY

"Success is not only measured by the accomplishments of the season but by the seeds you plant along the way."

1ˢᵀ HALF (OBSERVATION)

- What is my biggest fear as a coach?

  _____

  _____

HALF TIME (EVALUATION)

- How has losing contributed to me as a coach?

  _____

  _____

2ND HALF (PRAYER TIME)

Lord Jesus, regardless of the circumstances and battles I face you are my "peace giver". You died and shed your blood so that I may have peace. I humble myself before your throne and rely on your ability to see my through every situation. Amen.

DAY 12

Enduring the test

By Coach Perry Fletcher

"Blessed is the man who perseveres under trial, because when he has stood the test, he will receive the crown of life that God has promised to those who love him."

James 1:12

Every person with a functioning mind should have thoughts of accomplishments or a desired goal and/or dream to reach. I believe every individual born ought to have a dream. It is because of a dream an individual develops drive. From your drive, you are fueled to possess your destiny. As coaches and leaders, it is our task to help foster the dreams and goals of the ones we are leading. Many times our athletes fail to dream or fail to believe in their dreams because of the environment they live in. Instead of dreams, they are faced with nightmares. Usually, if the latter is correct, there will be opposition when you try to establish team goals and destiny for your club or organization. The real question is, "how can your athletes buy into team goals when they don't believe in their own individual goals".

I have discovered the derailment of dream possiblityis brought on by adversity. So many of our athletes come from dysfunctional homes and /or adverse circumstances that on the first sight of adversity, they are ready to abort their dreams. In some cases because of being exposed to so much failure, many individuals are afraid to dream from the fear of not succeeding. This behavior will lead to a nonchalant team or organization; which in turn evolves into underachievers.

In our textual verse, James understood that anyone who was seeking a crown or was destined for a crown would be faced with trials. These trials are the same as adversity. As coaches we must help those we are leading to know that the adversity that shows up in their lives is not to destroy their dream but to test their desire to achieve their dream. Notice James doesn't put any emphasis on the nature of the trial or the damage the adversity might present. He simply says persevere. Even as leaders, if we face adversity, its not for us to abandon what our heart has desired. We must be willing to persevere through the test; knowing that the reward of our dream is not in whether or not we passed the test, but whether or not we endured the test. I know it may come as a challenge, but we must be able to get our athletes to believe beyond the broken areas in their lives. Its not our job to hinder their dreams but to help them to achieve their dreams.

DAY 12

Enduring the test

By Coach Perry Fletcher

_____

_____

HIGHLIGHT PLAY

"It is because of a dream an individual develops drive. From your drive, you are fueled to possess your destiny."

1ˢᵀ HALF (OBSERVATION)

- Am I living out my dream?

    _____

    _____

HALF TIME (EVALUATION)

- In what ways do I help my athletes attain their dreams?

    _____

    _____

2ND Half (Prayer Time)

Lord God, when I face trials that seems to overwhelm me, hide me under your shelter. You are my Jehovah Machsi. You are my refuge, my fortress, my dwelling place, and my home. In you and in you alone, I find safety. Amen.

DAY 13

Balancing act

By Coach Perry Fletcher

*"One that ruleth well his own house, having his
children in subjection with all gravity."*

Galation 5:26

One of the hardest task as a coach is being able to balance family time with job time. Many people fail to realize the amount of time that must be invested in order to have a successful program. There are a number of family, marital, and personal relationships that suffer each year because of a coach's commitment to their job. So here's the million dollar question; is there a balance between the two? If you show impartiality to one, the other will suffer. In an ideal world, your family will collaboratively join you in your efforts as a coach to meet the needs of your team. However, this is not likely. If we follow the blueprint God left in the book of Genesis, we will see where he instituted the family before he did the church. What does that mean? If God saw it necessary to bring life to the system of family before the structure of church, then it is necessary for us not to put another system before the system of our family.

I know it's never your intention as a coach to neglect your family but with the demands and stressors of your work, it is easy to do. Generally a bad day at work lead to a bad day at home. It is so easy to become frustrated at work and carry the same frustration home; which tends to be channeled toward your family. This type of tension can drive invisible barriers between you and your spouse and or you and your children. Instead of using your home as a dumping ground for your frustrations from work, you must learn to use your home as a neutralizer. Your home should be a place that reminds you of how great you are and how much you have accomplished. If you fail to tend to the needs of your home, then not only will you suffer agitation on your job, but at your home as well. You must strive to maintain order and peace within your family. The love generated by your loved ones will gird you as a safety net for the disappointment you may encounter from the job.

DAY 13

Balancing act

By Coach Perry Fletcher

MEMORY VERSE: I TIMOTHY 3:4 (WRITE)

_____

_____

HIGHLIGHT PLAY

"Instead of using your home as a dumping grounds for your frustrations from work, you must learn to use your home as a neutralizer."

1ST HALF (OBSERVATION)

+   How do I balance my family and my career?

    _____

    _____

HALF TIME (EVALUATION)

+   In what ways can I involve my family in my life as a coach?

    _____

    _____

2ᴺᴰ Half (Prayer Time)

You, lord, are the creator of time. My prayer is that you guide me and show me how to keep my life in line with your word. At times, I may feel pulled in a million directions. At these times, holy spirit, direct my path in the way you would have me to go. Amen.

Use your gift

By Coach Perry Fletcher

"As every man hath received the gift, even so minister the same one to another, as good stewards of the manifold grace of God."

1 Peter 4:10

Accepting the task of leadership must be a response to a higher calling. With that being said, to walk in the life of a coach is to live a called out life. Whenever you live a called out life as your profession, it often requires an intense sacrifice. There are some individuals who aspire from birth to be coaches and or leaders, but there is another group that coaching chose them. I know there are times, especially at the end of the month when you receive your pay check, when the thoughts come in your mind that the work you do deserves much more compensation than what you receive. So, the first sacrifice you are engulfed with is having to be in a smaller tax bracket that what you would desire. This is a reality when the years you spent in college, attaining a degree to do what you are doing, could have been spent on a field yielding more dividends than what you are receiving. In a society where the cost of living supersedes the monthly wages, it's very easy to doubt and even experience depression from your financial outlook. In the midst of the reality that as coaches we may never be compensated monetarily for the gift we share with so many others, we must hold to our compensation in the harvest from the seeds we sew into the lives of others. There is no monetary value capable of replacing the value of saving a life, leading a life and inspiring a life. PRICELESS!!

Proverbs 18:16 declares a man's gift will make room for him and bring him before great men. What does that mean? As long as you are operating in your gift, God will always make room for you. There will always be plenty in the place of your lack.

Day 14

Use your gift

By Coach Perry Fletcher

Memory Verse: I Peter 4:10 (Write)

_____

_____

Highlight Play

"There is no monetary value capable of replacing the value of saving a life; leading a life, and inspiring a life. PRICELESS!!!"

1ˢᵗ Half (Observation)

+ Is my performance as a coach governed by the salary I receive?

_____

_____

Half Time (Evaluation)

+ In what ways has coaching rewarded me other than money for the job I do?

_____

_____

2ND HALF (PRAYER TIME)

Lord, you are the giver of all gifts. Empower me to use my gifts for your glory. You promised in me in proverbs 18:16 that my gift will make room for me. My prayer is that I will use my gift as a light to draw people closer to you. Amen.

DAY 15

You are the example

By Coach Perry Fletcher

*"Whatever your hand finds to do, do it with your
might, for there is no work or thought or knowledge
or wisdom in Sheol, to which you are going."*

Ecclesiastes 9:10

There are times in your career when the work you do will seem
small and in vain. It can become emotionally challenging to
consistently pour into people on a daily basis and not be able
to witness any results. As coaches, we must be careful that
our mode of instructing is not predicated upon the demeanor
of those whom we are leading. So many times, coaches and
or leaders will reduce their level of intensity because of poor
performance or a lack of enthusiasm from their team. This is a
coach's sin. You should never let your passion for what you do
be unfueled. You can't allow your player's attitude to dictate
your heart for what you do. You have to at all times possess the
greater influence within your program. Every now and then

you will be faced with a group where their slothfulness can be demoralizing. However, who you are as a coach, and everything you believe in as a coach is more valuable than an attitude of slothfulness. You must not allow your expectation for those under your leadership to be diminished by a lack of effort and energy from your players. You must lead and coach in a way that who you are as a coach will begin to transcend into your players or those you are leading.

Solomon pens in our theme verse that whatever our hands find to do, we must do it with all our might. In other words, there is never a time you should hold back. All of the knowledge and wisdom God has given you is no use in the grave. If you fail to give your all in what you do as a coach, when you die, every desire and every ounce of wisdom, every insight, every idea within you will be deposited into a grave rather than into a life. If it is in a grave that means it is buried but if it's in a life that means it's a blessing!

Day 15

You are the example

By Coach Perry Fletcher

Memory Verse: Ecclesiastes 9:10 (Write)

_____

_____

Highlight Play

"You can't allow your player's attitude to dictate your heart for what you do."

1st Half (Observation)

+ Do I coach to my potential or the potential of my players?

_____

_____

Half Time (Evaluation)

+ Do my players attitude resemble mine?

_____

_____

2ND HALF (PRAYER TIME)

Lord, you have equipped me to be the example before my players in a dark world. I ask that you give me wisdom to know how to lead. Holy spirit, teach and guide me to be a leader as you lead me. Amen.

DAY 16

Suit up

By Coach Perry Fletcher

*"Let us therefore cast off the work of darkness,
and let us put on the armor of light."*

Romans 13:12

To be without knowledge is considered to be in darkness. To without knowledge will not only have you in darkness but will cause you to lack motivation. Motivation stems from having the knowledge of attaining a particular goal. Therefore it is impossible to be self - motivated or to motivate others if knowledge is absent. It is a dangerous place to coach and or lead in darkness. If we consider darkness, the first thing it affects is your visibility. All coaches and leaders should have vision. If there is no visibility then there is no direction for those you are leading. There is nothing worse than to witness a program that's operating in darkness. What does that look like? There will be no team uniformity. Conduct of the team member will lack discipline. Attitudes will display arrogance. There will be no reflection of pride seen in the team's effort. Lastly, the overall program will lack respect for themselves individually and collectively as a team. There are no benefits found in darkness that will help aid you in success. Matter of fact, darkness will forever frown your visibility and keep you and your program stagnated. Nevertheless, there is an anecdote. It is called light.

Paul shares with us here in Romans when we cast off the work of darkness (laziness, selfishness, slackness, arrogance) then we will be open to light. What makes light so valuable? Take a second and close your eyes. Now open them. Now for a moment when your eyes were closed, you knew you were holding a book but you couldn't see the lines. Because you couldn't see the lines, you were unable to go on to the next passage. However, when you opened your eyes, you were able to pick up where you left off and move forward. What is the point - once your eyes were opened, you were exposed to the light. The light gave you the ability to see what you couldn't see in the darkness and move ahead from where you were. There is more. Because the light gave you the ability to move ahead, you were able to attain knowledge you didn't have before. This, my colleagues, is the advantage of operating in light. Light is symbolic of you having assess to knowledge. The more you know will give you the luxury of teaching those you are leading more. In the life of coaching, it's one thing to teach them a play (you go there, you go there, you do that) but in order to get more elusive results, we must teach them how to play. In order to reach this accomplishment, we must move from darkness and into the light.

DAY 16

Suit up

By Coach Perry Fletcher

MEMORY VERSE: GALATIANS 5:26 (WRITE)

_____

_____

HIGHLIGHT PLAY

"It's nothing wrong with being confident, but make sure your confidence stems from the hard work you put in and not the product that hard work puts out."

1ST HALF (OBSERVATION)

+ How do I handle success?

    _____

    _____

+ In what ways has being successful or unsuccessful effected my demeanor?

    _____

    _____

Half Time (Evaluation)

- What kind of example do I set for my athletes?

  _____

  _____

- Do those I'm leading show confidence or arrogance?

  _____

  _____

2ᴺᴰ Half (Prayer Time)

Holy Spirit, remind me that in order for me to be a true man/woman of God, I must "suit up" with your armor. The world's armor of arrogance or pride has no room in my life. Show me how to display the shield of faith so I can believe the impossible. Show me how to display the sword of the spirit so I can resist the devil. I chose to walk in the light of your word today. Amen.

DAY 17

Lord, I look to you

By Coach Perry Fletcher

"Look at the Lord and his strength, seek his face always"

1 Chronicles 16:11

Leading others can be very time consuming and become very demanding. In many instances, the weight of your responsibilities can and will suppress the life out of what you do. When the life of what you do is gone, you are now trying to function without strength. Having no strength in what you do, leaves you open to burn out. It's nothing worse than to witness a coach or leader trying to operate in leadership while experiencing burn out. Burn out is being overly fatigue, losing the will power to carry out your job assignment.

It is important to be aware and alert of stressors that can cause your strength to be depleted. Whether you realize it or not, it is a task trying to keep balance of an entire team. So often the pressure to win and to be successful carries a significant burden that is unnoticed. It's important to realize that in spite of what you have to be to so many others, you are still nothing more than a mortal. That means you are subject to fatigue and failure. The sooner you realize that your body has limitations, you can then begin looking to the strength of the Lord. Paul pens in II Corinthians 12:9, "and he said unto me, my grace is sufficient for thee: for my strength is made perfect in weakness. Most gladly therefore will I rather glory in my infirmities that the power of Christ may rest upon me.

WOW! Did you hear what Paul said. For those leaders who lead under the unction of God, in the moments where your strength is absent, Christ's power is present! Now it makes sense why Paul says he glory in his infirmities. In those times of personal disarray, you don't have to be disappointed. God will provide you with suitable strength that will succumb your situation. As leaders, we have to look beyond our attributes and focus on the strength of the Lord. His strength allowed a small lad to defeat a giant; His strength allowed on man and one stick to part the Red Sea; His strength allowed His Son to carry the weight of the world on His shoulder up a hill called Calvary. What you must realize is that you have access to that same strength. There is no reason to try an function in weakness when the strength of the Lord is available.

DAY 17

Lord, I look to you

By Coach Perry Fletcher

MEMORY VERSE: I CHRONICLES 16:11(WRITE)

_____

_____

HIGHLIGHT PLAY

"As leaders, we have to look beyond our attributes and focus on the strength of the Lord."

IST HALF (OBSERVATION)

+ When I'm overwhelmed, who do I look to for counsel?

    _____

    _____

+ How often do I have to be strong for others when I have no strength?

    _____

    _____

Half Time (Evaluation)

- In what ways can I avoid allowing my tasks to deplete my strength?

  _____

  _____

- How can I employ those I'm leading to be strength for each other and myself?

  _____

  _____

2ND Half (Prayer Time)

Lord, there will be days when I am frustrated, and I want to give up. However, I will choose to look to you when I think I'm worn out, burdened, or defeated. I will look to you because you are my Jehovah Shammah, the lord is there. Because you are here with me, I look to you and know that you have me in the palm of your hand. Amen.

DAY 18

Created to do good things

By Coach Perry Fletcher

*"For we are his workmanship, created in Christ
Jesus for good works, which God prepared
beforehand, that we should walk in them."*

Ephesians 2:10

Knowing who you are is instrumental in becoming the person
you desire to be. It's impossible to be something that you have
no knowledge of. There are a number of people living their lives
everyday as imposters because they have no true knowledge of
who they supposed to be. As coaches and/or leaders, it is easy to
govern your life on the basis of what you think is acceptable by
others. This logic will create faulty leadership which in turn will
develop a program with no identity. How can you help develop
someone else when you haven't been developed yourself. There
is an old expression that says, "the blind can't lead the blind.
In order to be productive and impactful, you must know who

you are. They only way this can be achieved, is by first knowing who created you.

In reference to our memory verse, we are the workmanship of the Lord, therefore we were created by royalty. When you realize the fashion you were created in, then you will know you are equipped with passion, purpose and promise. Too many people live their lives beneath their privileges because not only do they not know who they are, but they don't know who created them.

When you begin to learn of the one that has created you, you will better understand who you are. Just knowing that I am the work of the Lord adds a significant amount of confidence to who I am as a person. It's no way as a leader I can live a life and lead a life with no purpose when the Great Dispatcher of Purpose had created me.

DAY 18

Created to do good things

By Coach Perry Fletcher

MEMORY VERSE: EPHESIANS 2:10 (WRITE)

_____

_____

HIGHLIGHT PLAY

"How can you help develop someone else when you haven't been developed yourself?"

1ST HALF (OBSERVATION)

+ Who am I?

    _____

    _____

+ When others look at me, what do they see?

    _____

    _____

Half Time (Evaluation)

- Do I carry myself in the manner I was created?

  _____

  _____

- Are my actions a reflection of who I was created to be?

  _____

  _____

2ND Half (Prayer Time)

Lord, I surrender to you this day to do the work in me that needs to be done. Lord, show me what you have created me to be and to do. Amen.

DAY 19

Hope

By Coach Perry Fletcher

"The Lord is my portion, saith my soul;
therefore will I hope in him."

Lamentations 3:24

In order for you to survive, have energy, obtain vitamins, and receive strength, it's imperative that you eat the proper foods consistently. It is understood knowledge that humans are fueled by the diet of our choice. Because food is a necessity to live, being able to eat is a priority. Not only being able to eat but being able to provide and prepare to eat is a priority. So it is safe to say that food is your portion in order to sustain your physical body and have life as a human. In parallel to this logic, our theme verse says the Lord is my portion. Yes my dear brother and sister, just as food is your portion to survive as a human, the Lord must be your portion to survive spiritually as a leader. How so? If the Lord is your portion, that means you understand that your survival and success is contingent upon your consumption of the Lord.

So often our mental capacity is consumed with studying and researching different techniques and tactics to improve our team. In general, we are reading coaching magazines, watching videos, or anything to pick up new tools to enhance our system of play. In the shuffle of arming ourselves to be better coaches and leaders, often we neglect to arm ourselves to be better individuals. The same preparation it takes to develop a healthy coaching philosophy, it takes equal or more to help develop as a well – rounded spiritual being. We have to be mindful that if Christ is not a part of our diet, then our attitude as coaches will solely be governed by what we intake personally. This is not good. That means our philosophy, how we respond to situations and circumstances, and the attitude we display will only reflect the type of portion we receive in our daily regimen.

So in order to lead in a spirit of excellence, the Lord must be our portion. To be able to give out, you have to have something to draw from. If you never commune with the Lord, you will forfeit the opportunity to learn of his ways. According to scripture, His way is right, therefore to have him as your portion is the beginning of right leadership.

DAY 19

Hope
By Coach Perry Fletcher

MEMORY VERSE: LAMENTATIONS 3:24 (WRITE)

_____

_____

HIGHLIGHT PLAY

"To be able to give out, you have to have something to draw from."

1ˢᵀ HALF (OBSERVATION)

- ✦ How much reading do I do for personal growth?

    _____

    _____

HALF TIME (EVALUATION)

- ✦ Am I able to give leadership references to those I'm leading?

    _____

    _____

2ND HALF (PRAYER TIME)

Lord God, I cannot do anything without you. You are my hope and my portion. When tests and hardships come my way, remind me that my hope and faith is in you. I am encouraged that Psalm 62:5 reminds me, "Let all that I am wait quietly before God, for my hope is in him." Amen.

DAY 20

Believe

By Coach Perry Fletcher

"Jesus said unto him, if thou canst believe, all things are possible to him that believeth"

Mark 9:23

The successful key to any program is getting those that participate or those that follow to "buy in". This is an expression often used in the sports world to express that the participants believe in the teachings of the leader. It is impossible to build a winning program without having but in, if there is no buy in, those you are leading will never reach their individual potential. When those you are leading never reach their potential, your program will become stagnated. We are living in a generation now where people have a hard time believing beyond what their minds can ascertain. Maybe because we live in a society where individuals have to learn to be independent in order to survive due to the lack of support. It is important as coaches and leaders that we realize the culture of those we are leading. We cannot expect for someone to believe in our philosophy or logic when all they know is "me, myself and I". In order to accomplish "buy – in" when this type of attitude exist, you must challenge your followers to believe beyond what they can see.

In our devotional verse, there was a father who had a son who was possessed by an evil spirit. This father came to Jesus and asked could he heal his son. Jesus asked the man if he could believe that his son could be healed then it would be done. The man replied, "Lord, help my unbelief." What's fascinating is that even though this man came to Jesus for help, when Jesus offered help, the man still couldn't believe it. In the same sense, just because you have those following and listening to your instructions, doesn't mean they believe in what you are employing. In the text, this man said help his unbelief. As leaders, we must be willing to go beyond to assure that we reach buy-in amongst our team. According to our master, when there is buy-in, when we can believe, all things will be possible.

DAY 20

Believe

By Coach Perry Fletcher

MEMORY VERSE: MARK 9:23 (WRITE)

_____

_____

HIGHLIGHT PLAY

"We cannot expect for someone to believe in our philosophy or logic when all they know is 'me, myself and I'."

1ˢᵗ HALF (OBSERVATION)

+ Have I bought in to what I'm saying?

_____

_____

HALF TIME (EVALUATION)

+ What evidence do I see that those I'm leading have bought in?

_____

_____

2ND HALF (PRAYER TIME)

Lord, I must confess that at difficult times in my life, I have become discouraged. Because of life, I have questioned your love for me and my trust in you. Lord, forgive me and help my unbelief. I must believe you and your word. You are for me and not against me. I am willing to believe you over my current situation. I choose to believe you. Amen.

DAY 21

Your life is not only for you

By Coach Perry Fletcher

"The righteous who walks in his integrity –
blessed are his children after him."

Proverbs 20:7

In my earlier coaching career, I was blessed to be an assistant coach for the Men's program at Alcorn State University. While there, I recruited a young man named Almaad Jackson from Mesquite, TX. Recruiting Almaad was very instrumental to my outlook on coaching. The reason being, Almaad was an only child and his parents agreed to allow him to come over 7 hours to a school and state where he has no relatives. Upon his arrival the fall of his freshmen year, as I helped his father unload his things, I experienced a moment that was priceless and proved to be monumental to me as a coach. Mr. Jackson looked me in the eyes, shook my hand with tears streaming down his face, and said, "Almaad is the only son I got." I said yes sir and we are blessed to have him. He tightened up on my hand and said again, "Almaad is the only son I got." From the look in his eyes and the passion in his voice, I realized the subliminal message he was sending to me. In that moment, I realized that Mr. Jackson was insinuating that in his absence, he was holding me responsible for more than coaching his son but to stand in his likeness to cover his son. The analogy is that for the next four years, I would be involved in Almaad's life more that his own father. WOW! At 25 years of age, it hit me. My life, my attitude and my demeanor would be the example and model that would coin young Almaad into the man he would become. My actions could make or break him.

Coaches and leaders, by now you should realize that the role you play in the life of others is more than leading them to a championship or success, but it's about helping them to live a championship life.as coaches, in many instances we have more influence on our athletes than their own parents. This is partly because of the amount of time required in leading a successful team. When you think about having this much influence on an individual, Proverbs 20:7 should be your motivation. If we as coaches, walk in integrity, then those behind us will be consumed by the residue of blessings.

DAY 21

Your life is not only for you
By Coach Perry Fletcher

MEMORY VERSE: PROVERBS 20:7 (WRITE)

_____

_____

HIGHLIGHT PLAY

"Coaches and leaders, by now, you should realize that the role you play in the life of others is more than leading them to a championship or success, but it's about helping them to live a championship life."

1ST HALF (OBSERVATION)

- Do I lead out of obligation or justification?

_____

_____

HALF TIME (EVALUATION)

- After a defeat, what do those I'm leading look like?

_____

2ND Half (Prayer Time)

Lord, at times I lose focus on how I live and who is watching me. I must remember that my life is not only for me. Every day I affect lives in good or bad ways. I influence lives by my attitude, my decisions, my responses, and even my nonverbal messages. As I journey this thing called life, please guide me and instruct me on how to live my life. Amen.

DAY 22

Are you dull or sharp?

By Coach Perry Fletcher

"Iron sharpens iron, and one man sharpens another."

Proverbs 27:17

One of the loneliest journeys to be on is the journey of a coach. Many people on the outside looking in are led to believe that the lifestyle of a coach is filled with gleam, glamour, and glory. Not true. Although coaching and leading others can be rewarding, it also has it challenges. Often times as a coach, you are pulled in so many different directions until you struggle with who and what is genuine. It is a sad reality but every person that you meet does not have pure motives. In the field of leadership, predators will prey on you in order to benefit their very own selfish desires. That's why it's so important to have a relationship with God in order to possess a spirit of discernment.

Day 22

Are you dull or sharp?
By Coach Perry Fletcher

Memory Verse: Proverbs 27:17 (Write)

_____

_____

Highlight Play

"Although coaching and leading others can be rewarding, it also has it challenges."

1ˢᵗ Half (Observation)

+ Who has been the most influential person in my life?

_____

_____

Half Time (Evaluation)

+ Who have I influenced or poured into that in which was poured into me?

_____

_____

2ND HALF (PRAYER TIME)

Lord, I must remember that there are seasons in life. I may be in a season where I am the iron. In this season, I will be able to motivate another person. However, there may be another season where I must be the rock. In this season I may be needed to just sit and show someone how to wait on you. Instill in me your discernment. Remind me of my season and how you want me to use me. Amen.

Day 23

Jehovah shalom

By Coach Perry Fletcher

"The Lord shall fight for you, and ye shall hold your peace."

Exodus 14:14

Carrying the mantle of leadership is armed with a wealth of responsibilities that in many cases are not recognized and often overlooked. These responsibilities my dear colleagues will put you in some pressure situation. No one likes to talk about the pink elephant in the room but the reality is that the role of leadership whether you are coaching, teaching, parenting, or just living, can bring about times where you are subject to attack. In most cases, it's probably safe to say that as a Coach, we experience daily "battle moments" that are not handled right could lead to the demise of our career.

I can recall a time where it appeared that my boss had it out for me. Not sure of the reason, (ok, yes I am but that is another book) however, my boss really tried to put pressure on me and make my job much more difficult than it actually was. My boss called me in the office at 6:50 A.M. before the work day even started and gave me all these changes in my schedule that would take place immediately with no prior notice. I could have rebuttal but the Holy Ghost begin to translate my thoughts and my words. Instead of saying you can have this job, I responded Yes Ma'am. Can we take a moment, and tell God "Thank You"? Why? Won't he hold you when you can't hold yourself?

Alright, back to the story. I was puzzled to as why my boss could be so vindictive toward me when I only try to do my job. However, an hour after I had been hit with all of these malicious changes, the same pressure my boss was putting on me, was place on my boss. Look at God! Obviously, my boss didn't realize that although I was a coach, I also was anointed. (Psalms 105:15 – Read it at your leisure) It was that experience that confirmed that the Lord will and would fight your battle.

In our devotional verse, Moses was also faced with a battle moment. With Pharoah behind him and the Red Sea in from of him, I'm sure he assumed he was facing the benediction of his life. Can you say "Stand Still"? When what he was facing go to be too much for him to handle, God begin to handle what was handling him. Whenever you are facing battle moments, we have to learn to trust the captain that has enlisted us. He knows what we can handle and he awaits the opportunity to fight on our behalf. My fellow companions, the battle is not yours, it belongs to God.

Day 23

Jehovah shalom

By Coach Perry Fletcher

Memory Verse: Exodus 14:14 (Write)

_____

_____

Highlight Play

"When what he was facing got to be too much for him to handle, God begin to handle what was handling Him."

1ˢᵗ Half (Observation)

✦ What type of battles do the enemy present me with?

_____

_____

Half Time (Evaluation)

✦ How do I respond to opposition?

_____

_____

2ND Half (Prayer Time)

Jehovah Shalom, you are my peace. Persecution will come. Battles will be fought. Conflicts will emerge. However, through all of this, remind me that when I trust you that you bring peace to my heart and soul because I abide in your presence. Amen.

I've got to have faith

By Coach Perry Fletcher

"Knowing this, that the trying of your faith worketh patience."

James 1:3

One of the hardest principles to teach is how to advance through adversity. There are numerous strategies and coping and skills that can be acquired to be able to handle adversity but as coaches we must be able to equip those we are leading to not only be able to handle adversity but advance through adversity. The reality is that before you can model or employ this principle, God will often times allow you to live through it. It's a known fact that you can't teach what you don't know and you can't lead where you don't go.

In order to excel through adversity, you must understand the motives behind what you are facing. All adversity is not designed with evil intent. There are times that the adversity you face can actually be of more help than it is harm.

#1 – Adversity can bring you into humility. So often coaches can get sidetracked by the power of position that they lose a sense of self. Adversity has a way of displaying the reality that you are still human and no matter what your status may be, you are not above life.

#2 – Adversity will create hunger. When it is situations prevent you from attaining your goals, the passion within you won't allow you to succumb but rather strive. It is during your adverse moment as a coach you true character is tested and developed. In order to enjoy tea from a tea bag, it has to be put in hot water. Why? The hot water is what brings what's on the inside of the bag out.

The writer James offers us insight in verse 3, that when our faith is tried, when we encounter opposition, it's not all the time to destroy us but to develop us.

DAY 24

I've got to have faith

By Coach Perry Fletcher

MEMORY VERSE: JAMES 1:3 (WRITE)

_____

_____

HIGHLIGHT PLAY

"In order to enjoy tea from a tea bag, it has to be put in hot water. Why? The hot water is what brings out the ingredients on the inside of the bag."

1ST HALF (OBSERVATION)

+ How has adversity shaped my life?

_____

_____

HALF TIME (EVALUATION)

+ How can I use adversity in my position as a leader?

_____

_____

2ND HALF (PRAYER TIME)

Lord, Hebrews 11 also reminds me of the importance of faith. My faith must come from you and my trust in your word. Shift my mindset on how I view adversity. Allow me to embrace adversity because it will increase my faith in you. Show me daily that I must believe you above my circumstances. Amen.

Printed in the United States
By Bookmasters